For You
Teen-Ager
in Love

WALTER RIESS

Concordia Publishing House — Saint Louis, Missouri

To Lois, My Wife

And with thanks to
Larry Steyer, Youth Counselor,
for his suggestions

In These Talks with You . . .

For You, Teen-Ager in Love

Falling in love — and falling out of it again — are common experiences in the lives of almost all teen-agers, as they are in yours. This problem of love helps make adolescence the bumpy, thorny path that it is, even for Christian teen-agers.

Yet there is a glory in Christ, and a way of living in His church, that can carry us all over the roughest roads. And even though you think your particular love problems are the worst ever, our Lord knows what they are all about.

And your church has seen her people by the hundreds and the thousands pass through adolescence into the almost unbelievable happiness of true Christian marriage and home building.

So, please don't think of "going it alone." Your church is most warmly interested in you and your problems. And your love is not something to be ashamed of, or something to run away from, or something to hide. It is part of your Lord's plan for you, this love you have. And your church wants nothing more than to help you build that love into an even healthier and happier experience.

As editor of high school materials for a church, I have known many teen-age couples in love. Some of these couples built beautiful marriages on their love. But some did not. And I feel that those who did not might have listened, at least a little, if someone could have explained to them some of the things that strengthen love, and some of the things that at last destroy love.

This is the reason for this small book — to mark out some of the guidelines of love that our Lord and His church have given you. If you find for yourself just a page that will clear your mind a bit, or a paragraph that will show you the way to a happy Christian marriage, I will be happy with you. We will be happy together, in Christ Jesus, our Lord.

W. R.

All the Kids Are Doing It

How much "pressure" is on you to act, feel, and think a certain way?

"Pressure? Who, me? I don't jump for anybody! *Nobody* can pressure me!"

Right you are. You're a free American — with all the rights of the Constitution and the Bill of Rights behind you. You can't be pushed around. You'll be yourself.

But you aren't yourself — not quite.

You wear the same kind of clothes as the others in your class. You go to see the same movies, and you probably wouldn't set out for the concert if your crowd was going to the amusement park. You would worry a little, wouldn't you, if you got dropped from the party list, or if one of your friends started sniping at you behind your back.

9

You're an American, certainly you are. But don't deny it — you *are* under pressure to carry the ball just the way you are carrying it right now.

However, don't feel too bad about your inner urge to swing into line. Even the most mature adults realize that they have to conform — at least a little — with the world about them. That's why mature adults will be the last to laugh at teen-age bobby sox, hot rods, or cheer leader uniforms.

Yet when that social pressure to be like others grows too great, when you try *too hard* to be just like every other kid in your high school, you may be in for trouble.

Because God didn't make you that way — to become simply a wire in a huge computing machine, or a weather vane that spins with the wind every time it blows.

He made you to be a personality of your own.

Look around you in nature — and you won't see a single leaf just like another, or even a blade of grass that will match perfectly another, or one single pebble that will duplicate any other pebble on the beach.

Your personality, your looks, your gifts, your smile . . . the way you walk, think, speak . . . your athletic skills, your interest in a certain kind of work, to be done a certain way — all this is you, just you. And there's no one exactly like you, who can make exactly your kind of contribution, in the rest of the world.

You are you, and you alone, because you have a magnificent Creator.

He, too, is quite an individualist.

You must admit that the crucifixion of Jesus Christ is a unique fact in all history. Nothing else before or since can match it — not only because He was God's very Son, but because God chose this way (of all things!) to save us.

And look at the way Christ refused all His life to "go along with the crowd," to become a king with a throne, to pat the pious old Pharisees on the back and say, "Nice going, fellas, you just keep it up, and you'll get to heaven!" Nonsense!

Christ was Himself with everyone. And if, as the Bible says, He was "tempted as we are in all things," it wasn't always the easiest thing under heaven for Him to stay that way, either.

Like you. Like you in the corridor at high school, trying to avoid being swept along in the crowd like a branch in a rapids. Like you on a double date trying to dodge a drink when everyone else is saying chicken. Or like you in a parked car with a fellow you like, trying to keep his hands from wandering while you still want to go out with him. Not easy — any of it, is it?

But here you are, in America, in an American high school. And what do you do about it, to stay yourself, to keep some morals intact?

The answer?

This isn't easy either.

11

There is no answer — except *knowing yourself*.

Knowing yourself well enough to decide: This is the way I want to date, this is the way I want to study, this is the way I want to be popular, this is the way I want to live.

You are a person already. Now make yourself a person — with standards. With ideas. With insight.

You don't have to stain your morals to be popular. Don't believe it. You don't have to go steady to have boy friends, or girl friends. Don't believe that either. In fact (just on the QT), you'll rate a yard higher in everyone's book by stating your standards — and keeping them.

That is, almost everyone's.

But get this. The people that will not respect your standards as a person will not respect *you*.

That kind of person you want to avoid from a mile away.

Come to think of it, being an American means being free also to make up your own mind about your kind of life.

And being a Christian takes that meaning and stamps it out in gold, and etches it into rock.

Well, do you *dare* to be yourself?

I dare you!

If I Love Him, Why Wait?

I heard a girl say those words just a few months ago.

She had a lot of logic on her side too. She *did* love her fellow, and he loved her, and they had been going "steady" together for over a year.

He had every promise of a successful future — scholarship to a big Midwestern college, sterling-silver records at high school in basketball and baseball, friendly personality, enough brains to make a straight B average.

And she could make him a beautiful partner: looks, personality, zest for life — she had it all. She didn't want an education, felt she didn't need one. But she could go with him to college, couldn't she? She could keep house for him while he made good in his basketball scholarship, and she could be there waiting when he came home from road trips with the team.

13

Life looked rosy. Too rosy. So rosy no one could mention the other side. There would be money problems, for he had no income outside his scholarship. She could go to work, sure — until a baby came. Then what?

They married, just before he had to leave for college. For all of two months they found almost delirious happiness. And then the wedding money ran out.

Just about the same time, she learned she was pregnant. And at exactly the same time he learned what a college expected of a boy on scholarship.

For one thing, when you're on a scholarship, you have to *keep* grades high. You can't take night jobs. You study, or you risk losing the hand that feeds you. For another, you have to keep up something of a social life with the rest of the team, and with the alumni, and with all the people who consider you property of the school. You are expected to hang around the frat house, and you are expected to carry on like a freshman without a problem in the world.

But our young couple did have problems. And they suddenly found their early marriage pulling them out of the stream of college life.

That boy, right now, is facing the possible end of his education. Odds are that he'll have to find a job, leave school, and support his family. His young wife cannot work enough to pay the bills, buy the food, and still keep baby in care. Do you know what it feels like to doubt your marriage to the one you love?

14

— Or what it's like to look at your baby and feel you can't really give the little tyke the care he needs?

— Or regret that you didn't see *before you married* that all these worries could pile up on you and drain you of all the romance that once made your love so full of color and life?

To so many young couples today waiting seems almost like a denial of love, or faith, or hope.

But waiting can actually be a sign of higher, richer love. Waiting can mean — and often does mean — that your love is mature, ready to face the facts of daily life. Waiting can mean that you want *your* marriage to last a lifetime, and that you will settle for nothing less.

No one should ever tell you, or would want to tell you, that "marriage on a dime" doesn't have any chance at all. Plenty of couples have started on nothing but debts and made a go of it. But that kind of start does strain a marriage, even if it doesn't kill it. And do you really want to put *your* love under such a strain?

There are several questions you'll want to ask yourself before you take the leap of love. Let's list them together:

1. *What kind of life does my partner really want? Can he — or she — have that kind of life if we marry now, or will marrying block it off?*

2. *How much income will there be for us when baby comes?*

15

3. *Do we both have the kind of temperament and personality that can take strain without exploding?*

4. *Will we be able to live in a place all our own, or will we have to live with in-laws?*

That last question is a dilly. Life with in-laws may seem a delightful future now, but moms- and dads-in-law can seem like different people after the wedding day. To really blossom, your marriage has to have a quiet place all its own. You want to cut those apron strings with a sharp scissors. You want to shape your own way of life, even if it means drinking powdered milk on Saturdays to save your penny-wise budget.

Remember, in all this we're thinking of your love first, your future home, your children. How about you?

What are you thinking of, first?

If You Love a Girl, Petting's
All Right, Isn't It?

Waht a glinting, whirring gadget is the automobile!

Enough power to take you from home to highway to your high school's out-of-town game on just a couple dollars' worth of gas. Enough comfort to give you the feeling that you own the world. And enough privacy to be your own boss, away from prying eyes or loud voices that keep saying no.

And enough glamour to add oodles to any love affair.

It all adds up to a whale of a picture. You love your girl, she loves you. Day after day you manage to get together — at least for a few minutes, at least for a half hour. Night after night you can be alone together, in your own chariot, with no one to see or care what you do.

19

And, of course, if you love, you show it. If you love her very deeply, it's hard to keep from showing it not only with kisses and handholding, jokes and laughs and lighted eyes, but with necking and fondling and petting, and all of a sudden you are lost in a delirium of intimacy.

After all, who is hurt? If she loves you as much as you love her, why hold back? Isn't love the most perfect, the most exciting experience that can happen to teen-agers? Why snuff the experience, or risk killing it, by going puritan? How can you show love by acting as if you're afraid of passion, or by pretending you are holier than the next fellow with his steady date?

All this sounds logical — all of it makes sense — and all of it is very convincing — *but only so long as you think only of the body!*

There is certainly nothing unusual, or wrong, with admiration of a beautiful girl. And if you're lucky enough to have a beautiful girl in love with you, it is the most natural thing in the world for you to want to touch her, to show your admiration for her body.

But beautiful girls — and young men too — are made up of more than just body.

Hollywood and most of TV try to tell us that radiant face and figure are the only features in a girl you want to care about. Which is the main reason why marriages in Hollywood have the life expectancy of an eight-day clock with a broken winder.

That beautiful girl you admire, or even love, is a *person,* a *psyche,* a *soul.*

Her body makes just the smallest part of that person. She has emotions, feelings, desires, hopes, wishes, dreams, affections that you can never fully know. The part you see is like the peak of an iceberg on top of the ocean. Underneath the water, hidden beyond all sight, rests ten times that which lies on top.

But what has all this got to do with petting?

Well, that body is a little bit of a traitor to the rest of our *persons.*

Your girl wants to be a strong woman, someday. She wants to become a fine mother, a mother who can guide her children with all the wisdom and courage she can muster. She wants to keep herself for the man she eventually marries — just as she'll want her children to keep themselves for their marriage partners.

But the body doesn't always go along with the hopes, the prayers, of the person underneath. In fact, we'll say right here that, given the right kind of moonlit night, the soft music, and (remember chapter one?) the wrong kind of group pressure, many girls will give in and let a boy they like pet without too much resistance.

But afterwhile, when you've taken your girl home, her real self starts talking up again. Yours too, maybe! Civil war breaks out. And that civil war hurts every part of the person, breaks down self-confidence, maims integrity, and creates a bustle of confusion where once there was peace and honor.

We aren't even asking how far you go in your petting — if you're able to stop or not, or if you can wash this whole matter out of *your* conscience! We're talking now only about your girl, about the pain and confusion *she* will have to suffer — *especially if she likes you.*

If your girl is a Christian (and we hope she is), you may easily make her wonder about the strength of her faith or her morals. Do you really want this for her?

The more she loves you, the more torn she will be between her love and her devotion to her own principles. Do you want this for her?

Remember, she wants to become the finest person she can possibly be.

Wouldn't you like to help her?

Helping her might not seem as much "fun." But helping her — or any person — can be an adventure in Christian joy. It can be an adventure with your Savior Jesus Christ.

And if you do marry her — this girl so beautiful, so loved — you will find that petting then has a purpose far beyond anything you might know now. For the conception of a child is such a magnificent gift from God that no words can cover it.

We want that for you, both of you. Can you hold yourself

back, just a little, in preparation for the best years of your life?

Your Lord is here to help you. And your girl will be grateful for your strength . . . and your Christian thoughtfulness . . . and your concern for her.

But How Can I Be Sure?

For every teen-ager who falls deeply in love, wants to get married very soon, or knows "there is nobody else in the whole wide world," there are ten who suffer from inner confusion about their dates.

Usually it works this way. Either the boy or the girl puts on pressure for going steady, or getting engaged, or even getting married. The other member of the couple doesn't like to keep saying no. After all, you *do* lose wonderful dates that way! And usually this member of the party adds: "The trouble is, I do like him (or her) — but I don't know how much. I really don't."

Have you tried to paddle this boat lately? If so, don't think the world is coming to an end. You have more company than you dream.

You have company going way back to Plato, or Aristotle — and every other ancient philosopher who asked the question, "What is love?" You have loads of company in the Bible, even among people like David — who made the mistake of not distinguishing between love and lust. That's what caused all his trouble with Bathsheba and started the ruin of his entire house.

So . . . you're not lonely, all right? But let's talk it over, calmly and sensibly.

What is love, romantic love, of the kind that makes for happy marriages and happy homes that do not come apart at the seams?

Love is pretty hard to pin down any time, but here are some questions that can help you decide for yourself.

Do I know the faults of my partner?

The Hollywood idea of romance often doesn't take faults into account. And it's easy to write faults out of a movie script. Unfortunately, in real life everyone has a more than adequate supply of these uncharming pests — including your date.

If you've been able to face up to those faults, and still find yourself "in love," then you have moved from a Hollywood screen-story romance into a more real relationship with your partner. You have managed to get over a rather rough bump in boy-girl relationships — that first moment when you know your date is just as human as anyone else.

26

But if you're still so starry-eyed that your buddy seems like an angel knocked out of heaven fresh into your lap, look into the mirror. You may seem the same way to your date — and *you* aren't so angelic, now, are you?

This doesn't mean you have a poor romance. It may just mean you have a ways to go before you know what kind of romance you really do have. Wait till you get over that bump, and then take another look.

Can we "ride out" arguments?

If you've had arguments — and you probably have had more than one — what was the aftertaste like? Bitter, soured feelings for days? Or mutual let's-talk-it-all-out agreement, followed by more sweetness than ever before, and real appreciation of the other's character?

Arguments are a part of life, you know. If you don't have any at all, do you talk about important issues? Or do you duck them? Issues are like dandelions. They keep cropping up no matter how much you try to mow them down. The best way to handle them is to uproot them, bring them into the open, and meet them as they sprout.

If you can ride out arguments together, wonderful! If not, please take another look at yourselves. And don't let the dandelions grow under your feet!

Are we comfortable — even when we're not talking?

It's a thrill to be the life of the party — but parties always end sooner or later. And keeping up a constant line of patter can grow boring too, like a saw that never quits grinding. Do you feel, on a date, that you have to keep talking, that any silence means a ruined evening? Can you drive for miles and not say a word, and still feel that you belong together?

Married life means sitting in the living room together and saying nothing. It means long periods of delicious silence. If it means anything else but — if it means the hurried rush to the TV set, or the movies, or the night clubs, or the office — then marriage can strain terribly at the nerves of both partners. You'd be surprised how important it is *to be able to be quiet with the one you think you love.*

Do we like to go to church together?

Don't smile at this one. It's not just pious talk that worshiping together means a oneness you can't find any other way.

Having faith in common is probably the most vital connecting link between any two young people. For faith will hold when everything else gives way. But if a *together-faith* is missing, what in the world will keep a romance alive for all the years of marriage?

Many a social historian has pointed out that the early pioneer couples on the American frontier had more than just a love of fighting Indians to keep them going. Matter of fact, none of the girls then liked to face starvation and death any better than do today's brides. But those pioneer couples made a special effort to nourish each other's faith in a loving

28

Lord, a forgiving God, and in the future of a land where you could worship in peace and freedom.

Your life battles will be different than theirs. But you'll need the same armor.

Do we have a lot in common?

Somebody in the back row whispers, "Phooey! *We're in love!* That's enough in common, isn't it?"

No, it isn't.

Love, like hothouse plants, needs constant feeding. Thousands of couples get married every year who swear they're desperately in love, can't possibly spend a minute apart, etc., etc. This kind of confession is splashed on the pages of every issue of every movie magazine in the country.

Two years later, and what's happened to this "desperately in love" business? Why the divorce court? Why the arguments? Why the scandal?

Well, wifey had her movie career. Hubby had his yacht. Sometimes she was away for two months at a time. And he? Well, he loved the water, you see — and she just *hated* yachts!

Of course, there are a dozen other problems in a marriage like this. But why, we have to ask, *why* didn't wifey find out *before* marriage that future hubby was married to yachting? And why didn't hubby find out that wifey was already engaged to the movie camera?

Love cannot last without the nourishment of mutual interests, loves, hopes, backgrounds, and above all, faith. If you find yourselves constantly bickering about every little odd and end, arguing about what movie to see, which people to visit, what things to eat, whether to go swimming or hiking or skiing, whether to dress this way or that, whether to stay in or go out . . . quit fussing, will you?

Better find yourself someone a little more like yourself.

Can we talk about God together?

You are quite sincere in your faith, aren't you? (If you've read this far, you've proved that much to us.) You want to find out what God can mean in your life, not only for today, but for tomorrow and tomorrow and tomorrow. And you have every right to want that for yourself.

How about your partner? Does he, or she, feel interested enough in God to talk about Him? Or is the subject so out of reach for you that you are embarrassed together if a religious program should start pouring out of your car radio?

Don't fool yourself about this: God has a way of pushing everything else in life into second place. If that process is going on in you (and we think it *is*), you can't hide it from others without hiding yourself in the bargain. Anyone you can't talk God with is someone who will always be partly a stranger to you, no matter how hard you try to get through.

That's just the way this faith in God works in us. "For we," as Paul said it, "are ourselves living temples of the living

God, as God has said: I will dwell in them and walk in them; and I will be their God, and they shall be My people."

Make it that way always, will you? You'll find it's by far the best way for you to live . . . with or without that person you think you love.

What Is the Way of Christ for Me?

Once I asked a Christian teen-age boy, whom I had come to admire for his strength and purity of character, what made him so sure of himself in knowing how to treat a girl, where to take her, and what to do with her?

He said, "I remember the kind of life that Jesus lived. And," he added, "I pretty well know the kind of life I can have if I follow His lead."

That boy, not long after, married a beautiful girl and became a draftsman in a large city firm. He built a ranch-style home for his wife and himself, plus one rattling, red-cheeked baby boy, and always radiated that power of character that I had seen in him during his dating days.

But is it always that easy to know Christ's way?

One high school girl attending Bible discussion found it anything but easy to find Christ's way. "I get so confused," she said, "that I wonder how mixed up you can get in this kind of world. I honestly don't feel that the Bible helps me much, if any. Because after Bible class I go right on getting mixed up about what's right and what's not right."

Sounds familiar, doesn't it? And there are a lot of fine Christian young folks with the same story: "I'm all mixed up about right and wrong." "I don't know whether I'm any good or not." "What can you do with a person like me?"

Knowing "right" from "wrong" is often anything but simple. Look at the confident teen-age boy, and then at the confused high school girl, and you'll know that so many of us stand right between them.

Sometimes the way of our Lord appears so clear. And then — maybe the very next day, the very next date — we're lost again, in a muddle.

For instance, you make a date with a boy who seems a wonderful Christian to you. Yet he belongs to a Protestant church of another faith, and he's completely sold on that church. Gradually he tries to get serious with you, tries to get you to go steady. You feel you could easily love this young man. But what about the strain of different church memberships? What about the possibility of marriage — could it work out well for you under the circumstances?

What is the way of Jesus here for you?

There is no "outside" answer to that, is there? If you were

in this girl's shoes, you'd have to do your own thinking, your own praying, and your own deciding. You'd want to consider your parents' advice, your friends', and your pastor's.

But in the end the decision would be yours, and no one else's. And the way you chose to go would be, of course, the way you felt was the right way, the way of your Lord Jesus Christ.

Yet there are a few guidelines that may help you make the decisions that only you can make — and make them with an eye toward eternity.

Teen-age Christians who want to follow in the footsteps of Christ *can do it.* But . . .

1. *Please — please! — avoid any activity that puts your bodily emotions in charge of your spirit. Don't let your love for Christ ever take second place to "passion pit" experiences.*

2. *Think of your Bible as the Word of God, and treat it that way. Then let the thought sink in through the hours:* My faith is based on the inspired Word of God itself!

3. *Confess your love for Jesus when you pray.*

4. *Be willing to take whatever He sends. Like John the Baptist, you humble yourself that He may be exalted.*

5. *Set your heart to love all people, even those who don't like you. If you really love your date, you won't do anything to hurt his, or her, spiritual life.*

These five guidelines, I think, may well explain the strength of the teen-age boy whose story started this chapter. He had a devotional life with Christ — based on firm habits with the Bible and prayer — that kept him clear-eyed in every situation.

Can you be that sure of yourself, through Christ?

Well, there will always be problems that make it hard to light up the straight and narrow way that the Lord wants for us.

But there will also be the light of Scripture to brighten our eyes and clear the shadows from the path ahead.

Trust that. Build your devotional life, and your vision will start to clear. And you will be strong.

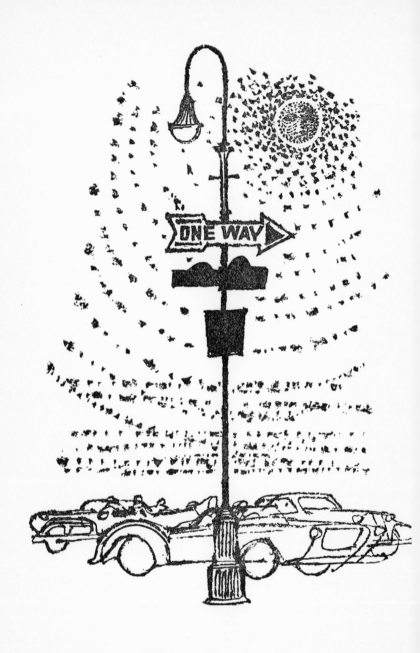

I Go Steady — And I've Got Dates!

That's like saying, "I've got a lifetime pass on the street car — and am I going to travel!"

You'll travel, all right — but only to this end of the line, or that end. The tracks stop, and there's no place to go, and you may be stuck at the end of the line.

You have dates, sure you have! The same fellow, the same girl, that you saw last night or the night before or the night before that. Are you in love? How do you know — you haven't really given yourself a chance to find out.

Of all the new-fangled pills that American teen-agers have swallowed, this going-steady cure is the worst ever. The only thing it cures is date insecurity. And it doesn't even really cure that.

You may think it does. If you find yourself going to pieces the moment you have to face a basketball game without a date, or a prom night without a partner, then you may grab at the going-steady tonic like a drunk heading for the tavern. It heals everything, doesn't it? Johnny keeps coming over, keeps ringing the doorbell. And all you have to do is — yes, that's right — all you have to do is *keep convincing yourself that there isn't another person in the world you'd rather be seeing.*

Do you believe yourself?

Not that some "steadies" don't make out. They do. But they may — just *may* — be making out in spite of, not because of, the "steady" business. For don't you ever wonder whether it's smart to slam all the doors on everyone but one particular person before you're actually sure *in yourself* that this person is *the one?*

There are three times in your life, say the wags, when you make the newspapers — no matter who you are: when you're born, when you get married, and when you die. You can't do much about being born, and you can't control the end of your life. But you *can* meet people, a lot of people, in preparation for the years upon years that you may spend with some other person.

It's especially important to talk about this now, at a time when "teen-age divorce" keeps popping up in the magazines. So many of these stranded and brokenhearted teen-agers open up their past with a single confession: "I just didn't meet enough kids before I got married." "We weren't really sure."

These teen-age divorces reveal how really serious a matter it is to tie yourself down to one person. God may have ever so many sparkling happinesses in store for you. He may be leading you toward the most thrilling dates you could dream of having. But you can block all this out. You can let your own insecurity drive you into going steady with someone you aren't yet sure about, someone who may *or may not* be the right person for you. And so you can cancel out your own future happiness.

Luckily — luckily for you and many other teen-agers, going steady simply doesn't hold anchor when the wind starts rising. Jenny may swear by Roger — until one day she gets a smile from that new boy in the school hall. Roger may not know it, but he's about to lose a steady.

"Lucky!" you complain. "This kind of stuff breaks hearts!" And so it does, for a while at least.

But when would you rather have your heartbreak — before or after marriage? Before or after children come?

When would you rather sit out your lonely nights — before or after marriage?

It's a question you have to answer for yourself.
But before you decide for or against going steady, think of three other parties:

Your Lord, first Love in your life.
Your future life partner, and how you may meet.
Your future home, and what you want it to be like.

Your move.

Make it the right one, will you?

For Those Who Have Gone Too Far

It starts with a hesitant knock on the door. Or with a halting attempt at "light talk." There may be one teen-ager there, or two, and then, of course, the counselor. And he knows what is almost certainly coming. But he must wait and go along with the light talk. He knows the young people are gathering courage.

Then, finally, one of them draws it out into the open — a secret that has been smoldering at the bottom of their persons for who knows how long, smoldered there and created pain that only the teen-ager talking can estimate. And then, the blurted confession: We went too far.

Usually, the story has the same background — a parked car, a drive-in movie, or a party with a few drinks, a petting session, a feeling that "we simply couldn't stop," and a momentary sense of relief and pleasure. And for days on end, worry and regret and fear.

There may be a pregnancy. There sometimes is. But even if there is none, there is the same worry and regret and fear in any teen-ager who has any idea of what the Christian life can be.

"Now we feel terrible — and, pastor, we just don't know what to do. Our parents — we couldn't tell them. We came to you. . . ."

It is a terrible, aching thing to have guilt in your heart. The pastor knows this. Yet he knows also that the only way to remove guilt is to bring it out into the open, where it can be faced with something much more powerful, much more lasting. And so he asks a question that he hates to ask, because for a moment he must rub salt into an already sore and festering wound. He says, "You both know that you did wrong, don't you?"

And this is the hardest of all, to admit that love can take a wrong direction. After all, can't love be free — freely given and freely taken, and no questions asked? Can't love move without being harried and frustrated by laws, restrictions, or well-drawn lines?

The answer, of course, is no. Love can't be free — not as long as love involves more than one person and can hurt more than yourself. And love can hurt. Look at the young couple sitting now in the pastor's study, feeling the salt being rubbed into their wound, feeling for the first time in their lives, perhaps, the sharp bite of the Law.

"Yes, pastor. I think we know we did wrong."

It is the young man speaking, a dark-eyed, black-haired, not-quite-handsome fellow. His companion shows the truth of his remark in her eyes, wide eyes, and alert to danger that she hasn't sensed before. She is asking herself: *What will come of all this? Will this destroy our love?*

Perhaps the pastor senses her terror. For he starts to feel anxious to help her, to help both of them with a hasty use of his Gospel.

But there are other reasons for the pastor's haste to offer his Lord's forgiveness.

He knows — and he loves this fact — he knows that Jesus Christ Himself was quick to forgive people enmeshed in sins of the flesh.

There is that remarkable story of the woman dragged to Him after being caught in the very act of adultery. Her accusers gather around like vultures over a dying man in the desert. Their law says she must die. What would this impudent Christ — who called Himself the "Son of Man" and the "Son of God" in one breath — what would He do now?

What He did was so magnificent, so perfectly filled with grace, that to this day we can hardly believe He could be so driven by love.

"He straightened Himself up and said to them, 'Let the one among you who has never sinned, let him throw the first stone at her.'

47

"Then He stooped down again and continued writing with His finger on the ground. And when they heard what He said, they were convicted by their own consciences and went out, one by one, beginning with the eldest until they had all gone.

"Jesus was left alone, with the woman still standing where they had put her. So He stood up and said to her, 'Where are they all — did no one condemn you?'

"And she said, 'No one, Sir.'

And then some of the most healing words in all the Bible: *" 'Neither do I condemn you,' said Jesus to her. 'Go home and do not sin again.' "* *(John 8:7-11, Phillips)*

Who can forget the picture of this lonely Galilean and the frightened, trembling woman, and the soft sound of His voice as He forgave her everything?

Anyone who knows Jesus knows this picture is real, knows this voice is real.

Do you know Him that well?

You can. For He wants you to hear Him say *to you* again and again: "Neither do I condemn you. Go home and do not sin again."

You see, He does love you. And you can count on that — which is about the biggest thing to remember in your life.

Saying Yes at the Right Time

Purity has fewer defenders than ever among today's high school girls. A third of them, judged by their own statements, not only don't want to stay virgins, but *don't*. Not a few others don't want to, but do — quite possibly out of guilt feelings, or out of fears of pregnancy.

But statistics can be the smoothest liars in the world. And no one would want to impute to Christian young men and ladies the Kinsey data. Dr. Kinsey, after all, had no special interest in studying *Christian* youth (who, if they live according to Scripture, form a people called apart to the Lord). Obviously, the statement that eighty per cent of American brides age 22 have lost their virginity before marriage could not be used to shame the morals of our church youth.

But we ought to admit frankly that being Christian has not

freed us from the tug of a Kinsey-crazy society. Dr. Kinsey may not have known it, but in publishing his studies he gave a whole pad of excuses to a whole range of excuse-hungry adolescents.

Then, of course, there is the brand of psychologist (not every brand, by a long shot) who claims that to repress sexual impulse is to risk damaging your personality. According to him "safe" intercourse — with the use of contraceptives — "eases" young people into "mature" sexual relations after marriage.

What this brand of psychologist conveniently forgets while he advises sexual looseness is that our very civilization is built on *some degree of repression.* Modern psychology has proved also this — that man carries around in himself every kind of bitter hate, fear, jealousy, desire, and lust. What — we would like to ask — what if all these were allowed to roam free as a bird? What would happen to our cities? Would you like to walk in them if people suddenly quit repressing?

Also ignored by this kind of psychologists:

1. *Guilt feelings — which come to* almost everybody *who commits adultery;*
2. *The chance of having a child* in spite of *using contraceptives (none of them is perfect);*
3. *The wall this adultery builds in later marriage.*

What wall?

Well, what does free-and-easy lover boy tell his wife after marriage? If he is like most men, he will not want to marry any girl who has "played around." So . . . he marries a girl who has managed to keep her purity intact. But there are conversations, there are questions. There always are. And how do you go about tearing down a cellophane wall that the past has built between you?

And what will you tell your children someday when they reach adolescence? "Don't repress yourself, Sis — it might injure your personality"? I'll bet.

Somehow, purity never goes out of date. The more some fellows ridicule the gentleman, the more he stands out. The louder the laughs at the girl with standards, the finer her dates. And while many a Rome is burning down because of sexual looseness, many a young couple is building a future home out of clean dreams, smiles filled with love, the holding of hands, the goodnight kiss, and the wish to respect each other's freedom.

Freedom, that's right. For sex without restraint is nothing but a tyrant of a habit, a slave driver who will not stop until all purity and peace have been driven off. But sex with purity, sex with love, sex with respect — well, there's nothing so lovely in the world as a Christian honeymoon. No one so fair as a Christian bride. No one more gallant than a Christian gentleman who sees in the body of his beloved the indwelling Jesus Christ.

This is your dream, isn't it? Sure it is. For you wouldn't in all the world trade your birthright of purity for a porridge of guilt and regret. Yes, love. Yes, show affection. But let no one possess you until you have said your final happy "yes" before the altar of your Savior.

You are His, first, aren't you? *"Do not, then, allow sin to establish any power over your mortal bodies in making you give way to your lusts. Nor hand over your organs to be, as it were, weapons of evil for the devil's purposes. For sin is not meant to be your master — you are no longer living under the Law, but under grace."* (Rom. 6:12-14, Phillips)

And that's the only way for you to live at all.

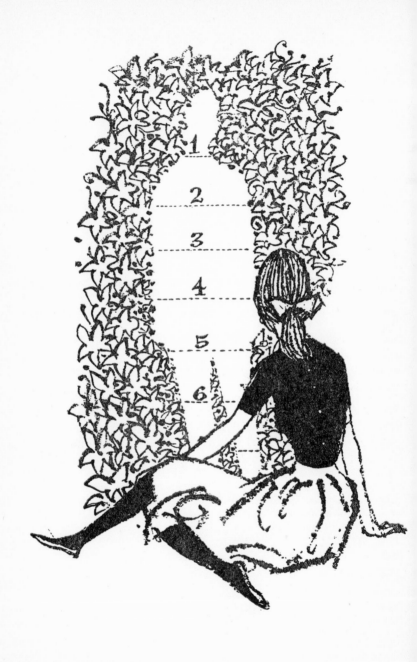

If You're Looking for Perfection

She was a startlingly beautiful woman, almost middle-aged, with an unmistakable talent for singing. After her concert at the church her pastor asked her, quite frankly, why she had not married.

She smiled with just a faint touch of regret showing in her eyes. "No man," she said softly, "is good enough for a young girl who expects perfection. I have learned since that I am as much a sinner as anybody. I guess," she admitted, "I could be more patient now."

There is, really, such a thin line between setting high standards for yourself and being proud.

It is one thing to say, "I want my romance and marriage to stay on the highest level. I want to find the most attractive, most sympathetic, and most high-principled partner I can."

All this can be said in humility. Or it can be said in perverted pride.

And there is the rub — not in the hopes, not in the wishes, but in what lies behind the hopes and wishes.
What is pushing you toward the best, the finest? What is driving you to strive for the perfect?

It's so easy to congratulate ourselves on high moral standards, so comforting to tell ourselves, "You really *have* drawn the line, my friend." If anything, this self-backpatting was the distinguishing mark of the Pharisees. It was so jolly cozy to stand on the street corners and catch the admiring stares, the ohs and ahs, the telegraphed admiration.

What kind of husbands do you think the Pharisees made? Would you like to know any of them too well?

Self-righteousness makes boring company. The prude on the date, the fellow who can't move unless every hair is in place, or the girl who has to change three times a day at camp, may think they are making a hit with the crowd. But actually, they are arousing suspicion. They are sending out radar signals reading: "Watch me, I think I'm something special." And people catch signals like that.

Nobody's special, and everybody's special — at least that's the way it is in the church.

"For all have sinned and come short of the glory of God" (Rom. 3:23). *"There is none that doeth good, no, not one."* (Ps. 14:3)

And yet: *"God commendeth His love toward us in that, while we were yet sinners, Christ died for us."* (Rom. 5:8)

Every single one of us who believes in Jesus Christ as Lord and Savior must face himself in the light of those two beacons —

1. *Universal sin;*
2. *Complete and saving grace.*

These beacons allow no room for pride.

They cut like lightning through the kind of wheezing self-righteousness that sets us up as better than anyone else.

But just as sharply, those beacon lights knife through below-standard morals.

Christ didn't die for us so that we could live in shadows. He didn't redeem our bodies so that we could roll around in the muck of human slime. He didn't redeem our minds so that we could smirch them in dreams and delusions of adultery.

"He died for all," Paul points out to us, "that they which live should not henceforth live unto themselves, but unto Him which died for them and rose again." (2 Cor. 5:15)

That is high-standard living.

That is life at its fullest, its clearest, and its most rewarding level.

That is life at its most perfect.

But remember, your Christian partner — with all his or her faults — is perfect in the eyes of your Lord Jesus Christ. Sinner? Yes. But also saint — just as you are sinner and saint.

Don't ignore either sin or sanctity. And try to like even the people you could never, never marry. God has a plan for you — but the plan *always* includes love, His and yours.

What If I Don't Get Married?

Take one girl, add one mother, stir in one prospective young gentleman, and you have a sure-fire recipe for "romance." It always works, because next to love, fear is the strongest emotion we carry around with us.

And fear of spending our lives alone can often knock us into the arms of the first buddy who pours out a liquid smile. Our heart melts (amply warmed on mother's flame), and we quote the old saw with new meaning: "A bird in the hand is worth two in the bush."

The only trouble is that we aren't getting married to a bird. It might be a lot better that way, come to think of it. Because birds don't talk back. But people do — especially after they discover we haven't been entirely square with them.

Many a "steady" beau — like, for instance, Andy — wanders around in a milky daze after suddenly discovering that Margie loves him "madly." But whenever Margie goes to a party with him, her eyes start roving like a city hunter on his first day in the woods. She shines like a new moon and reflects every sunny lad who notices her. Andy, of course (poor Andy!), doesn't know he's a bird in the hand. Not yet, that is. But just wait.

Andy's bound to catch on. Margie doesn't know that yet, but she ought to. And when Andy does catch on, chances are he won't catch on with his mouth closed.

Andy will be comparing notes. With other boys — lots of them. Some of them have gone out with Margie. Some of them already know she's eager for the altar, regardless of who walks her there — just so long as it's a male and her daddy to help steady her toward the marriage of the century.

Margie is a bundle of fears, really, in spite of her giggles.

She has fallen head over heels for the stale matron's fable that life alone is to be dreaded above tarantulas. Therefore: Get married, my daughter, at all cost.

Margie will, all right. Sooner or later someone a little dumber than Andy will come along the track like a streetcar and pick Margie up and cart her off and never see that Margie has marry-go-round eyes.

So ends the fable. Let us leave Margie to her so-so marriage, and take a look at the ancient American spinster-bachelor fables.

Years ago, when the Wild West was being settled by pioneers with square-wheeled wagons, becoming a widow was enough to make a girl commit suicide. For how — just how — could such a girl make a living? There were no offices that hired girls, no factories even, no place a girl could go alone without stares, and no clubs she could join.

Often enough — which was too often — such girls felt they were forced to take up highly questionable occupations just to get daily bread for themselves, much less to feed a baby or two. There actually were barroom gals like the type currently portrayed in TV westerns, but these girls didn't just go into the business for the fun of it. Where else, as we asked before, could they possibly go? Home to mother — if there was a mother and if she had a home. Sometimes she didn't.

And so, over the space of years, American men learned to wonder about girls without husbands. And girls began to wonder about girls without husbands. Guilt feelings started to simmer even in perfectly pure widows. And young ladies, feeling this embarrassment, started to make up their minds to "get married or bust." Most of them got married.

What the girls then didn't know, and didn't maybe care to think about if they did know it, was this brace of facts:

1. *There are slightly fewer boys than girls; so some girls must remain single.*

2. *Remaining single no longer meant going to work in a tavern, since society opened honorable doors to the unmarried lady.*

What the girls also didn't know, or didn't care to admit, was the obvious fact that some of them — not many, but some — simply weren't interested in marriage. They wanted to go into nursing, or office management, or writing. They would be bored to tears with cleaning a rug or bringing Dad his slippers. Some of them proceeded, because of the old American myth about unmarried girls, to get bored to tears. But that didn't help matters any. All it did was steal away men who might have made good husbands for some girl who *wanted* marriage — and wanted it above everything else.

The bachelor never had such a problem as the widow. All he needed was a horse to carry him from one town to the next, a six-gun to help him drive cattle, and a canteen for water. No one asked him questions about his married life, if any. For some queer reason or other, history has always treated the bachelor with kid gloves, and the unmarried lady with iron fists.

Today the iron has become cotton. For the resourceful unmarried girl, with the blessing of the Lord, can build a vibrantly creative life. If she doesn't care for marriage, she can rise as high as ambassador to a foreign nation, or state senator, or a novelist who talks to millions. She can make herself indispensable in an office, or she can nurse hundreds to health as a nurse, or build the church directly as a deaconess.

What if you don't get married? First, ask yourself if you want to. If you do, then hie yourself off to places where you'll meet the kind of men you want to know. If you don't,

62

withhold yourself from swallowing the old American myth, the old fears of being alone.

You are never alone. Not as long as you serve people in love. Not as long as you bear witness to Jesus Christ. All the loneliness of lonely people cannot stand before the warm and rushing drive of love . . . for all.

We Don't Need to Have the Same Faith

Churches change us in the strangest ways.

You can go to church almost all your life and hardly hear a word. A pleasant sleepiness can steal across your brow the moment you step into the narthex, and your rest can reach its peak by the administration of the usual sleeping pill, the sermon. If it weren't for the standing parts in the church service, you could relax all the way and forget that you were ever there.

At least you might think you could.

Couples try it every year, at a thousand altars, and sometimes with the blessing of the pastor.

After all, what does a difference in faith mean when all the world is hidden in your bride's eyes or your bridegroom's smile? Thoughts of churches fade into merciful haze, faith becomes all tangled up with physical love — until after the honeymoon.

Then the surprise hits home — the realization that your particular church, its patterns of worship, its faith emphases, have meant more in your life than you could possibly have dreamt.

And now you wake up, after marriage, to the fact that this faith difference affects every part of your life with your mate. *What do we read for family devotions? What table prayers do we say? How can we build each other's faith in a crisis? Will our child be given a Christian education? Where? Which pastor will we call on for counseling?*

Psychiatrist Louis Linn and Chaplain Leo W. Schwarz spotted these pitfalls in their book, *Psychiatry and Religious Experience*. "It is unfair to argue," they say, "that the concern of the church stems largely from its fear of losing members. While it is true that persons contracting mixed marriages tend to drop away from their respective churches and are more or less indifferent to the religious rearing of their children, there is another and more important reason for the church's stand in the matter. *It is that interfaith marriages are likely to be unstable.*

"Unfortunately," the doctor and the chaplain continue, "the young are impatient of the verdict. 'We are broad-minded,' they say. 'We are quite willing to respect each other's religious beliefs.'"

But respect is not sharing. And marriage is not marriage without sharing. And all the love at first sight in the world will not break down the glass wall between a husband and a wife deeply committed to separate faiths.

What are the usual reasons for marrying a person of different faith?

There are always reasons — reasons hidden far beneath our conscious mind.

There is a bit of the rebel in all of us — and marrying a person of another faith gives us such a sterling-silver chance to prove our independence over against our parents, our teachers, or our pastor.

There is the seeming necessity of finding a mate. In a time when staying single beyond twenty-five is touted as bordering on the old-maidish, young people can hurry themselves into almost any kind of match. And into almost any kind of divorce court. The fear of remaining single — sometimes foisted on the girl by mama — can act like a whiplash on an otherwise cautious and faith-conscious young lady.

But sometimes, sometimes, mature love is the reason. And sometimes this mature love will bring two people together who can actually contribute to each other's spiritual growth. This can seldom happen if the two faiths are miles apart — say, like the Roman Catholic, Christian Science, Jehovah's

Witnesses and the Lutheran, Methodist, Baptist. But two Protestants can possibly find, in their mature love, that ideal of sharing spiritual values until both find the same way, truth, and life.

In mentioning the Roman Catholic faith, it would be wrong to forget two factors that make a marriage between a Roman Catholic and a Protestant almost doomed to failure:

The Roman Catholic prenuptial agreement, wherein the children of the marriage are promised to the Roman Catholic faith.

The fact that the Roman Catholic Church does not regard as valid any marriage involving a Catholic which has not been performed in a Catholic ceremony under special conditions set by the Catholic Church.

It is impossible to overestimate the grief caused in some homes by those two factors. To live the rest of your life under such a contract, a contract involving even your children, is the best homemade purgatory you can invent for yourself. Mixed marriage is always a risk, always something to take to your Lord Jesus in prayer.

If you love Him first, and *then* whoever it is you're dating, you will be able to keep your P's and Q's straight as far as your future marriage and children are concerned.

Your Lord is involved here. And your church. And your future home. And even your future children.

And especially you.

What Marriage Is Really All About

P. T. Barnum never sold anyone such a fraud as the fraud
the "glamour" sellers have sold us — an image of marriage
as gaudy and cheap as the Golden Calf, and just about as
good to drink when chopped up and served to the public.

Magazine stands take the Golden Calf and parade it to the
people, to you, and to me, beating out a constant tattoo
upon our senses. The drums never stop beating: Marriage
is sex. Marriage is the bulbous bathing Miss America falling
in love at first sight with the Charles Atlas he-ro. Picture
magazines send their shutterbugs to Los Angeles night clubs,
and catch the Miss Americas and the Charles Atlases right
at their tables, just itching to fall in love.

The divorces are not mentioned in the picture legends. Why
spoil the fun? The left and lonely children of these mar-

riages — don't mention them! The alcoholics and dope addicts and sex perverts produced by this system of love and romance and marriage — hush! This is the Great American Way. It's already sold, and you can't do much to stop it.

Not even for yourself? Certainly we don't have to buy this product, hook, line, and sinker. It must be possible to duck this brand of marriage ideal and find something much different, much better.

Not entirely.

You and I cannot run out on the times in which we live. We're part and parcel of the culture which the entertainment industry has spoon-fed to us now for a quarter century. And that's a lot of spoon-feeding.

The very way you look at a person of the other sex, what you expect to do when you're out on a date, where you go, how quickly you "fall in love," the way you pooh-pooh "out-of-date" advice from mom and dad, the speed you drive your car, the hopes you have for your marriage — all these ideas are tinged by tawdry Hollywood chrome, whether you like it or not.

Which is why Christians have to be on their guard and etch on their minds clearer than ever before *what Christian marriage is really all about!*

Let's start where Hollywood ends up — at the intimate sexual relationship which is heralded as the final goal of marriage. Is that sexual union a goal, or isn't it?

Yes, it is — but not in the way Hollywood says it is!

"And they twain shall be *one flesh,*" Jesus Christ Himself said, and Matthew and Mark recorded it. And ever since even Christian people have sometimes felt that the Lord was pointing to the flesh as the be-all and end-all of marriage. For Christ went on to add: "Whosoever shall put away his wife and marry another, committeth adultery against her. And if a woman shall put away her husband and be married to another, *she* committeth adultery." And all this under Christ's real theme: *"What therefore God hath joined together, let not man put asunder!"* (Matt. 19; Mark 10)

By now you're a long way from just talk about flesh. You are facing a *union of persons* — so made *by God,* and made *so complete and final,* that separation is out of the question.

Now obviously, Jesus couldn't be thinking that two people would join themselves together flesh-wise all their lives. That would be a physical impossibility. What Jesus therefore meant by "flesh" was what we would mean by "personality." He was saying that a boy and a girl in marrying joined their personalities in such a way that to try to "get out of the marriage" would be sinning. Jesus said, in His typical picture language, that the boy and the girl were becoming *one person in body, mind, soul — in every way and in every part of their beings.* They were sharing — sharing perfectly and wonderfully — in the most miraculous union of two becoming one!

Jesus was far ahead of the modern psychologists when He spoke of "flesh" that way.

Today we know that it's impossible to separate body from soul, or body from mind. What hurts the mind hurts the body too. And the pain that attacks your flesh can — if you let it — undermine your very faith.

When you "love" a girl's body, or a boy's manly biceps, you should love that person's soul too. If you don't, you aren't really loving at all. You are simply giving yourself a thrill.

Which is all that happens in so many love-at-first-sight marriages. Falling in love with looks can be done in a split second, almost faster than you can say, "I do." But falling *out* of that kind of love can take only half a split second, or less time by far than it requires to buy a ticket to Reno.

But learning to know another person's thought-life, his or her ambitions, fears, dreams, hopes, attitudes, background, hobbies, takes more than a split-second effort. It may take six months; quite possibly more than a year. Sometimes it may take you two or three years until you are ready to unite yourself in marriage — the marriage of flesh and mind and soul and all your personalities — for a lifetime of living together.

There is no room in your lifetime for a ticket to Reno. There is no room in Christ's words to you for a hasty marriage, based on a "Well, if it doesn't work out, I can try again" philosophy. You can never try again without bearing scars much deeper than any flesh wound.

When you think of marrying a person, think of joining your innermost souls, your most intense secrets, your most hidden selves. And think of joining these in the name of Jesus Christ, at the altar of your church.

There you'll hear the words again: "What therefore God hath joined together, let not man put asunder." . . . "And they twain shall be one flesh."

And there, at the altar, you'll just begin to understand the full meaning of what Christ was saying.

And it will take you the rest of your life to understand the rest.

The Kind of Friend for You

The closest friend of teen-agers can be Jesus Christ.

But so many of the high school folks will not take Him along on the most important times of their life — on their dates, for instance, or to their parties.

There seems to be an ogre in all of us that tries to keep God in one corner of our lives. Mark that corner "Church," or "Sunday School," or "Christmas," or "Easter," and you have it tabbed.

But when it comes to the joy rides we prize most highly, we shove God even farther back into His corner and run off with the crowd.

Do you have any idea why this happens? Have you ever thought seriously about it?

We sing "What a Friend We Have in Jesus" — but we wouldn't think of letting His company butt in on our friendship with "the fellas and gals."

What kind of friend is He to us, then?

And there's another question we have to start asking ourselves.

What kind of people are the fellas and gals we run around with?

Do they have anything to do with our keeping Christ in a corner?

What would happen if, on your next double date, you happened to start talking about your personal faith in Jesus as your Savior?

Would you find ears listening? eyes ready to see? Or would you likely be slapped back with something like: "Get a load of the creep! Talking religion on a night like this!"

Your answer counts. Because your answer reveals not only what your friends are like, but *whether you can really open up your heart to them about the most vital part of your life.* Being friends is a lend-lease arrangement. You have to be able to take, but you also have to be able to give. And if you can't give to your "friend," you will want to ask yourself how much of a friend he — or she — actually is.

Of course, you can try to lead a double life.

You can ask your Father in heaven to give you Christ as the light of your life. And then you can go on being afraid to let that light even glimmer when you're out on the town.

But notice what's happening to you if you choose this course.

You receive light for your life — and then you snuff it out, hold it back, keep it from showing.

And all this for the sake of "friends" who will not hear you out about Jesus Christ!

How long can you do this without snuffing the light itself?

When will the time come when you find yourself no longer asking for Christ to be your life's Heart and Light?

"I tell you," He said once, "that every man who publicly acknowledges me, I, the Son of Man, will acknowledge in the presence of the angels of God. But the man who publicly disowns me will find himself disowned before the angels of God!" (Luke 12:8, 9 Phillips)

There's a challenge for you.

Enough of a challenge, it is, to lead you to test your friends, to speak His name whenever the occasion is right for it — to take Him along *all the way, all the time.*

Do you think this will harm your friendships or shadow your fun?

Not on your life.

If your friends can't stand hearing about the Lord of your life, they aren't your friends. And if they like to talk about the meaning of His Gospel with you, your life will take on a new radiance, a new excitement.

It's this kind of person-to-person Gospel witnessing that shocks all dullness out of life and brings you face to face with the most amazing realization of all — one that we need to bump up against a thousand times a lifetime:

He is here. My Lord is here. And I am never alone.